AF575201

A Portrait of Grinnell

The Architecture and Landscape of Grinnell College

to Hannah –
Best Wishes
David Kennedy

Plate 1 - Bucksbaum Center for the Arts in Winter

A Portrait of Grinnell

The Architecture and Landscape of Grinnell College

Photography by David K. Kennedy

with a foreword by David G. Campbell

100 Books Publishing Company

Dedication

To my parents, Sharon and Keith Kennedy, for teaching me to see the world for the amazing and beautiful place that it is.

Contents

Plate 2 - Tree & Carnegie Hall at Night

Foreword

David G. Campbell

The 82 compelling photos in David Kennedy's *A Portrait of Grinnell*—each capturing but a few hundredths of a second to, at most, a second or two—are instances that will never occur again. In sum they comprise a total of about seven minutes…that's just shy of a quarter millionth of the eight semesters that a student spends at Grinnell College. Evanescent, perhaps, but each image teaches us an important lesson about living and about seeing. There is a timeless and enduring grace in every moment of our lives, in every precious breath, as there is in every one of David Kennedy's photos. Each is a gift, each is epiphany.

How many times have we walked across our home campus, beneath a fissured oak that had spread its bough over generations of students and teachers, through the old brooding buildings and the upstart modern ones, past a spray of cone flowers as young as summer, under the vault of restive sky that, above all else, seems to define Iowa…and been too harried, too test-stressed, or preoccupied with petty hassles to notice these gifts? How many uncountable moments of grace have transpired and expired around us without anybody taking the time to pay homage to them? We train ourselves to be scholars, to inter pret the arcane, to think. But some of the truest lessons are as abundant and as free as the wind and the light. We need only to pause, and to praise.

Of course, it took David Kennedy years of practice to learn how to recognize those moments, and years of training to capture them in thin film or on silicon wafer. A photo, after all, has no objective truth. It is a human artifice, a facsimile of reality that is an alchemy of photons, fiber and pigments…and in the end, judgment: sensing what works—that's where the art resides. Like all art, a photo is a covenant between creator and viewer, and like all artists, the photographer must understand his species, how its mind works, its traditions, what resonates in ways that are primal and often subliminal, and what doesn't.

Over the years, I'm sure, *Portraits of Grinnell* will become one of your most cherished possessions. Each time you journey through these pages you will see our campus in startling new ways. Some of the photos will become as familiar to you as the faces of old friends.

Savor every page, pause, reflect…and learn to see anew.

Plate 3 - Noyce Science Center & "The Zirkle" at Nigl

Plate 4 - South Campus Path at Twilight

Author's Note

David K. Kennedy

I graduated from Grinnell College in May 2006 with a degree in history. By that time, what had begun as a modest hobby twelve years before, when my dad put a camera in my hands on my tenth birthday, had become my passion. For six out of my eight semesters at Grinnell I was the photo editor of the campus newspaper, *The Scarlet & Black*, as well as a photographer for the alumni publication, *The Grinnell Magazine*. More than this, for four years I walked across campus with a tripod over one shoulder and a camera bag slung over the other.

The unpredictable Iowa weather patterns presented a never-ending source of photographic opportunities. The old, paradoxical saying among photographers is: "bad weather is good weather." This book is a portrait of campus in its various moods—a bright spring day, a rainy afternoon, the first snow of winter, a cool fall night.

In the spring of my junior year, as a capstone for my work with the art department's Epson 9600 wide-format fine art printer and the guidance of Matthew Kluber, I held an exhibition of eighteen of my campus photographs at the John Chrystal Center. Entitled "In Response to Place," the show was my first exploration of the connection between people and their surroundings. I incorporated this idea into the artist's statement:

Some say that the people make a place, but I believe that the place itself shapes the character of those who inhabit it. I would ask viewers to consider this as they view these photographs and in so doing they might recognize how this campus has uniquely affected them.

This book represents a second, more comprehensive study of the way this campus changes everyone in its association, just as the campus itself transforms with time.

*****

Nothing in this world is accomplished without the help of others, and this book is no exception; my work is founded upon the love, friendship, support, fidelity and patronage of so many people. Foremost, photography would not have become my vehicle for artistic expression without my dad.

Kevin Pearson, Bob Sagadin, and my other teachers and advisers from The Prairie School in Racine, Wisconsin, have my thanks for their support.

I would not have begun to share my photography with the greater Grinnell community—let alone publish this book—had it not been for the persistence of Jeffrey Phelps and Mindy Bacon at Saints Rest Coffee House & Art Gallery. Henry Wilhelm and Carol Brower's enthusiasm at the opening of my first exhibition at Saints Rest in 2004, as well as their continued interest, has been a great source of encouragement.

Matthew Kluber and Bobbie McKibbin have been tremendous inspirations and advisers. The interest of Sam Rebelsky, Lesley Wright and Sarah Purcell has meant a great deal to me, and I am forever indebted to Daniel and Jill Kaiser for their support. This book would not have been possible without the generous help of Pete Brownell and Keith Kennedy.

These four years were made richer by my friends, who have all seen me at my best *and* worst, and carried me through to the finish. I do not know where I would be without Katie Mears '03, Emily B. Anderson '04, Meghan Kirkwood '04, Lara Gaasland-Tatro '04.5, Warren and Anne Claflin '05, Aly Beery '05, Abel Lomax '05, Chad Marzen '05, Eric Morris '05, Nick Santiago '05, Jenne Beinart '06, Laura LeVon '06, Anna McNulty '06, Margaret Toomey '06, Avi Pogel '06, Grant Woodard '06, Carolyn Voss '07, and especially Elizabeth Pekarek '05.

Finally, I am grateful that David G. Campbell pulled me aside back in August 2004 and had me see that my photographs were more than dots of ink on sheets of paper, but art that succeeded in connecting to its viewers.

--David K. Kennedy

Spring 2006

A Note on "Wide Format" and "HDR"

There are two components to every medium of artistic expression: the art itself, and the craft that enabled it to come to fruition. For the past twelve years I have refined my technique to capture my vision of the world with the great precision. I believe that there is a great deal of truth to the saying "garbage in, garbage out," and that digital capture is no excuse to become sloppy with technique ("I'll fix it in the computer"), but is actually an opportunity to yield even better results than were possible with film.

Thirty-five millimeter has been my format of choice for capturing my photographs, and for good reasons. Affordable, portable, compact and accessible are only some of the adjectives that explain why all of my images on film were captured using 35mm equipment. Each photographic format offers its share of advantages when compared to the others; medium and large format affords great scalability of prints at the expense of greater bulk and weight, whereas 35mm provides portability as well as greater depth of field (without resorting to camera movements)—while sacrificing the ability to make very large, grain-free prints.

In the summer of 2003, I transitioned from chrome to digital capture and acquired a six megapixel Canon 10D. As noted at the end of this book, most of my photographs have been captured with that body using RAW format for the greatest possible quality.

In the past I had scanned all of my slides and then processed them digitally, but an all-digital workflow has opened up a world rich with creative possibilities replete with the benefits of a histogram for a light meter and the gratification of immediate results.

The majority of the images in this book were shot on a tripod with a bubble-level, by using mirror lock-up and, to quote Michael Reichmann (www.luminous-landscape.com), by "exposing to the right." That is, I took advantage of the greatest quality offered by the digital sensor by exposing such that the resulting histogram reached the "right," or brightest end of the spectrum displayed. Digital sensors are linear devices and are broken up into approximately five stops of data roughly described as "blacks," "darks,"

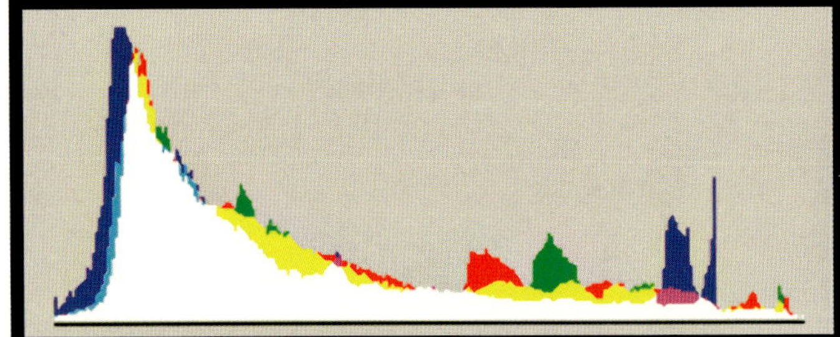

Histogram demonstrating a dark subject that has been exposed "to the right" such that details that would normally be compacted to the extreme left (blacks) spread out towards the right. Data has expanded entirely to the right (whites) without overexposure (compression on the right).

"middle tones," "light tones" and "whites."

The sensor captures twice as much data in the darks as it does the blacks, twice as many middle tones as darks, twice as many light tones as middle, and twice as many whites as light tones. Exposing for the brightest tones yields a decided advantage as it soaks up the most data possible per image and allows for greater flexibility in post-processing.

*****

One method of interpreting the world that has always fascinated me is panoramic or "wide format" photography. Wide format photographs have never had one "correct" formula for their capture; any image can be cropped for a "wide" interpretation. The freedom to crop and scale a photograph without compromising its integrity is directly related to the size of the original.

Digital 35mm camera bodies have leveled the playing field as it is now possible to capture a large, highly detailed wide-format image from a 35mm digital body that rivals a cropped photo from a body or camera back of a larger format or a greater megapixel count. A large photograph can be achieved by "stitching" multiple images together. To create a wide format image from multiple captures seamlessly requires additional equipment, software, patience, and stable environmental conditions

Wind, rapidly changing clouds and sunlight can foil even the best attempts at a "stitched" image. Equally important is the control of parallax, which requires either the use of a lens with a tripod collar, a lens with shift movements, or specialty equipment to change the center of rotation from the

A Note on "Wide Format" and "HDR"

camera body to the entrance pupil of the lens. *(See the illustration of the difference in panning from these two distinct centers of rotation.)*

When the camera body is panned while it is at the center of rotation, the mounted lens will "swing" to the left and right, thus altering the distance from the objects in the frame. Not surprisingly, slight changes in the position of the lens can radically alter the locations of compositional elements within the frame. Two objects that are distinct from one another may suddenly overlap with the gentle pan of the camera when the entrance pupil of the lens changes positions—hence the need to rotate from the position of the entrance pupil.

To correct for parallax I use a "nodal slide," a metal rail that I purchased from **Really Right Stuff** that enables me to cantilever the camera from the tripod so that the lens becomes centered over the ball head. I then process my RAW captures with identical exposure settings, and then put them together in specialty software, **Realviz** Stitcher Express.

There are ten "wide format" photographs in this book; each image spreads across two pages and is composed of at least three individual captures. Additionally, some of the photographs are actually two or three images that have been captured at different "shift" positions on my Canon 24mm tilt/shift lens and pieced together in Photoshop to yield highly detailed horizontal and vertical photographs that are free of parallax.

*****

Another technique that is represented in this book is "High Dynamic Range" photography. The human eye has far greater tonal latitude than does film or digital capture, so while the eye can reconcile the differences between a brightly illuminated subject and its unlit background, film or digital can only capture the bright subject and render the background very dark or even black. To increase the dynamic range, at least two exposures of a composition, differing only in exposure time (not aperture value), can be blended together to provide an image much closer to that delivered by the eye.

Top view of the difference in panning without (left) and with (right) a nodal slide to align the entrance pupil of the lens over the center of the tripod head to eliminate parallax. Note the changes in lens positions.

Photoshop CS2 provides the ability to blend many bracketed exposures into one High Dynamic Range (HDR) image.

Even with its relatively limited dynamic range, photography has obviously succeeded as an art form, so not every image captured must describe the scene as does the human eye to be a powerful image.

However, there are times when the ability to expand the dynamic range is a useful tool. The photographs that I have produced using this method are described at the end of the book (in Exposure Data) as having a shutter speed of "HDR."

Plate 5 - Bucksbaum / Faulconer Gallery Loading Dock

fall

Plate 6 - Alumni Recitation Hall (ARH) Gargoyle

Plate 7 - Looking Up at ARH

Plate 8 - ARH at Night

Plate 9 - Carnegie and Bicycle

Plate 10 - Steiner Hall at Sunset

Plate 11 - Steiner Skylight

Plate 12 - Steiner, Late Afternoo

Plate 13 - John Chrystal Center at Twilight

Plate 14 - Chrystal Center, Main Stairway

Plate 15 - Goodnow Hall

Plate 16 - Goodnow and Fall Color

Plate 17 - "Morphosis" by Rico Eastman, 6th Ave. & St. Paul's Church

Plate 18 - Noyce, Sunburst

Plate 19 - Noyce and Younker Hall

Plate 20 - Noyce at Night

Plate 21 - Herrick Chapel at Night

Plate 22 - Central Campus Tree at Night

Plate 23 - The Forum in Fall Color

Plate 24 - The Forum and Burling at Night

Plate 25 - Burling & South Campus in Mist

Plate 26 - Haines Hall in Mist

Plate 27 - South Campus Loggia

Plate 28 - Trees hanging over South Campus

Plate 29 - Verdant South Campus

Plate 30 - Mears Cottage

Plate 31 - Mears Cottage, Porch

Plate 32 - Rose & East Hall

Plate 33 - Lazier Hall Sunset

Plate 34 - Rose Hall Vestibule & "Remember the Seed Germ" c-prints by Sally Kuzma

Plate 35 - Rose Hall at Night

Plate 36 - Aurora Borealis over Mac Field (7 Nov. 2004)

Plate 37 - North Campus Loggia at Night

Plate 38 - Ganesha on a Rainy Day

Plate 39 - Read Hall in Winter

winter

Plate 40 - Central Campus Trees in Winter

Plate 41 - Goodnow in Snow

Plate 42 - Goodnow & Roberts Theatre in Snow

Plate 43 - Bucksbaum at Night

Plate 44 - Roberts Theatre Loading Dock

Plate 45 - Flanagan Theatre Loggia

Plate 46 - Impression #1, "Hat Trick" by Patrick Dougherty

Plate 47 - Impression #2, "Hat Trick" by Patrick Dougherty

Plate 48 - Burling in Light Snow

Plate 49 - Burling at Night

Plate 50 - Central Campus, the Forum on a Day without Snow

Plate 51 - Noyce & Construction Crane at Night

Plate 52 - Noyce, Central Campus in Snow at Night

Plate 53 - Noyce "Elbow" Ceiling

Plate 54 - Noyce "Elbow"

Plate 55 - Noyce Stairway

Plate 56 - Central Campus at Night

Plate 57 - South Campus after Snowfal

Plate 58 - Haines in Snow at Night

Plate 59 - Loose and Read in Snow

Plate 60 - James Hall in Snow at Night

Plate 61 - South Campus Winter

Plate 62 - Gates Tower at Sunrise

Plate 63 - "Early Morning Riser" / North Campus Loggia after Sunrise

Plate 64 - Clark Hall on a Winter Morning

Plate 65 - North Campus Loggia on a Winter Night

Plate 66 - Smith Annex & Langan Hall at Night

Plate 67 - Gates Tower in Snowfall at Night

Plate 68 - North Campus Winte

Plate 69 - Darby Gym (Razed 2004)

spring

Plate 70 - South Campus Trees & Haines Hall

Plate 71 - South Campus Coneflowers

Plate 72 - Late Afternoon Light on South Campus

Plate 73 - Lazier Hall in Spring

Plate 74 - East Campus Loggia #1

Plate 75 - East Campus Loggia #2

Plate 76 - Coneflowers and Bucksbaum

Plate 77 - Bucksbaum & "Morphosis" from 6th Ave.

Plate 78 - Herrick Chapel

Plate 79 - Trees, Benches and Noyce

Plate 80 - "Alpha and Omega" Sundial and Coneflowers

Plate 81 - Darby Gym in Winter

exposure

Exposure Data

Plate #	Title	Year	Camera Body	Mode/Film	Lens	Shutter Speed	Aperture	ISO
1	Bucksbaum Center for the Arts in Winter	2005	Canon EOS 10D	RAW	Canon 24mm f/3.5 L T/S	1/15 sec.	f/16	200
2	Tree & Carnegie Hall at Night	2005	Canon EOS 10D	RAW	Canon 24-70mm f/2.8 L	30 seconds	f/10	100
3	Noyce Science Center & "The Zirkle" at Night	2004	Canon EOS 10D	RAW	Canon 70-200mm f/2.8 L	25 seconds	f/29	200
4	South Campus Path at Twilight	2004	Canon EOS 10D	RAW	Canon 70-200mm f/2.8 L	4 seconds	f/8	400
5	Bucksbaum / Faulconer Gallery Loading Dock	2005	Canon EOS 10D	RAW	Canon 24-70mm f/2.8 L	1/40 sec.	f/16	100
6	Alumni Recitation Hall (ARH) Gargoyle	2003	Canon EOS 10D	RAW	Canon 100-300mm f/4.5-5.6	1/20 sec.	f/11	100
7	Looking up at ARH	2003	Canon EOS 10D	RAW	Canon 28-80mm f/3.5-5.6	1/20 sec.	f/11	100
8	ARH at Night	2005	Canon EOS 10D	RAW	Canon 24mm f/3.5 L T/S	20 seconds	f/10	400
9	Carnegie and Bicycle	2003	Canon EOS 10D	JPEG	Canon 28-80mm f/3.5-5.6	1/125 sec.	f/7.1	100
10	Steiner Hall at Sunset	2005	Canon EOS 10D	RAW	Tokina 12-24mm f/4	1/15 sec.	f/22	400
11	Steiner Skylight	2002	Canon EOS Elan 7	Fujicolor Super HQ (C-41)	Canon 28-80mm f/3.5-5.6	unknown	unknown	100
12	Steiner, Late Afternoon	2005	Canon EOS 10D	RAW	Canon 24-70mm f/2.8 L	1/25 sec.	f/22	400
13	John Chrystal Center at Twilight	2005	Canon EOS 10D	RAW	Canon 24mm f/3.5 L T/S	2.5 seconds	f/11	400
14	Chrystal Center, Main Stairway	2002	Canon EOS Elan 7	Fujicolor Super HQ (C-41)	Canon 28-80mm f/3.5-5.6	unknown	unknown	100
15	Goodnow Hall	2003	Canon EOS 10D	JPEG	Canon 28-80mm f/3.5-5.6	1/100 sec.	f/7.1	100
16	Goodnow and Fall Color	2005	Canon EOS 10D	RAW	Canon 24mm f/3.5 L T/S	1/40 sec.	f/18	200
17	"Morphosis," 6th Ave. & St. Paul's	2005	Canon EOS 10D	RAW	Canon 24-70mm f/2.8 L	1/80 sec.	f/16	200
18	Noyce, Sunburst	2005	Canon EOS 10D	RAW	Canon 24mm f/3.5 L T/S	HDR	f/20	100
19	Noyce and Younker Hall	2004	Canon EOS 10D	RAW	Tokina 28-70mm f/2.8	5 seconds	f/8	200
20	Noyce at Night	2005	Canon EOS 10D	RAW	Canon 24-70mm f/2.8 L	13 seconds	f/11	400
21	Herrick Chapel at Night	2005	Canon EOS 10D	RAW	Canon 24mm f/3.5 L T/S	2 minutes	f/22	200
22	Central Campus Tree at Night	2004	Canon EOS 10D	RAW	Sigma 12-24mm f/4.5-5.6	20 seconds	f/8	200
23	The Forum in Fall Color	2004	Canon EOS 10D	RAW	Sigma 12-24mm f/4.5-5.6	1/13 sec.	f/22	100
24	The Forum and Burling at Night	2004	Canon EOS 10D	RAW	Canon 70-200mm f/2.8 L	4 seconds	f/8	400
25	Burling & South Campus in Mist	2004	Canon EOS 10D	RAW	Tokina 28-70mm f/2.8	10 seconds	f/11	200
26	Haines Hall in Mist	2004	Canon EOS 10D	RAW	Canon 70-200mm f/2.8 L	3.2 seconds	f/8	400
27	South Campus Loggia	2004	Canon EOS 10D	RAW	Tokina 28-70mm f/2.8	1/4 sec.	f/22	200
28	Trees hanging over South Campus	2004	Canon EOS 10D	RAW	Canon 50mm f/1.4	1/50 sec.	f/7.1	400
29	Verdant South Campus	2005	Canon EOS 10D	RAW	Canon 24-70mm f/2.8 L	1/4 sec.	f/22	400

Exposure Data

Plate #	Title	Year	Camera Body	Mode/Film	Lens	Shutter Speed	Aperture	ISO
30	Mears Cottage	2005	Canon EOS Elan 7	Fujichrome Sensia (E-6)	Canon 24mm f/3.5 L T/S	unknown	unknown	100
31	Mears Cottage Porch	2005	Canon EOS 10D	RAW	Canon 24-70mm f/2.8 L	1/100 sec.	f/11	200
32	Rose & East Hall	2005	Canon EOS 10D	RAW	Canon 24mm f/3.5 L T/S	1/60 sec.	f/22	100
33	Lazier Hall Sunset	2003	Canon EOS 10D	RAW	Canon 28-80mm f/3.5-5.6	1/125 sec.	f/8	400
34	Rose Hall vestibule	2005	Canon EOS 10D	RAW	Canon 24mm f/3.5 L T/S	1/8 sec.	f/22	200
35	Rose Hall at Night	2004	Canon EOS 10D	JPEG	Canon 28-80mm f/3.5-5.6	2 seconds	f/9.5	100
36	Aurora Borealis over Mac Field	2004	Canon EOS 10D	RAW	Sigma 12-24mm f/4.5-5.6	1.25 minutes	f/8	200
37	North Campus Loggia at Night	2003	Canon EOS 10D	RAW	Canon 28-80mm f/3.5-5.6	4 seconds	f/8	200
38	Ganesha on a Rainy Day	2004	Canon EOS 10D	RAW	Canon 70-210mm f/3.5-4.5	1/3 sec.	f/25	400
39	Read Hall in Winter	2004	Canon EOS 10D	RAW	Canon 20-35mm f/3.5-4.5	1/100 sec.	f/10	100
40	Central Campus Trees in Winter	2005	Canon EOS 10D	RAW	Canon 24mm f/3.5 L T/S	1/125 sec.	f/11	400
41	Goodnow in Snow	2005	Canon EOS 10D	RAW	Canon 24mm f/3.5 L T/S	1/30 sec.	f/16	200
42	Goodnow & Roberts in Snow	2005	Canon EOS 10D	RAW	Canon 24mm f/3.5 L T/S	1/15 sec.	f/16	200
43	Bucksbaum at Night	2004	Canon EOS 10D	RAW	Canon 20-35mm f/3.5-4.5	3.2 seconds	f/5.6	100
44	Roberts Theatre Loading Dock	2005	Canon EOS 10D	RAW	Canon 24-70mm f/2.8 L	1.6 seconds	f/8	400
45	Flanagan Theatre Loggia	2005	Canon EOS 10D	RAW	Canon 24mm f/3.5 L T/S	1 second	f/11	400
46	Impression #1, "Hat Trick"	2005	Canon EOS 10D	RAW	Tokina 12-24mm f/4	HDR	f/11	100
47	Impression #2, "Hat Trick"	2005	Canon EOS 10D	RAW	Tokina 12-24mm f/4	HDR	f/11	100
48	Burling in Light Snow	2005	Canon EOS 10D	RAW	Tokina 12-24mm f/4	1/10 sec.	f/16	200
49	Burling at Night	2005	Canon EOS 10D	RAW	Canon 24-70mm f/2.8 L	20 seconds	f/11	200
50	Central Campus, Forum w/o Snow	2006	Canon EOS 10D	RAW	Canon 50mm f/1.4	1/125 sec.	f/10	100
51	Noyce & Construction Crane	2005	Canon EOS 10D	RAW	Canon 24mm f/3.5 L T/S	3.2 seconds	f/11	400
52	Noyce, Central Campus in Snow at Night	2005	Canon EOS 10D	RAW	Canon 28-135mm f/3.5-5.6 Image Stabilized	30 seconds	f/16	200
53	Noyce "Elbow" Ceiling	2004	Canon EOS 10D	RAW	Canon 20-35mm f/3.5-4.5	1/15 sec.	f/8	100
54	Noyce "Elbow"	2004	Canon EOS 10D	RAW	Canon 20-35mm f/3.5-4.5	1 second	f/10	100
55	Noyce Stairway	2004	Canon EOS 10D	RAW	Canon 20-35mm f/3.5-4.5	2 seconds	f/10	100
56	Central Campus at Night	2006	Canon EOS 10D	RAW	Canon 24mm f/3.5 L T/S	HDR	f/8	400
57	South Campus after Snowfall	2005	Canon EOS 10D	RAW	Canon 24-70mm f/2.8 L	1/10 sec.	f/18	400
58	Haines in Snow at Night	2005	Canon EOS 10D	RAW	Canon 28-135mm f/3.5-5.6 Image Stabilized	30 seconds	f/8	200
59	Loose and Read in Snow	2004	Canon EOS 10D	RAW	Canon 20-35mm f/3.5-4.5	1/100 sec.	f/9	100
60	James Hall in Snow at Night	2004	Canon EOS 10D	RAW	Tokina 28-70mm f/2.8	8 seconds	f/8	100
61	South Campus Winter	2004	Canon EOS 10D	RAW	Tokina 28-70mm f/2.8	8 seconds	f/8	100

Exposure Data

Plate #	Title	Year	Camera Body	Mode/Film	Lens	Shutter Speed	Aperture	ISO
62	Gates Tower at Sunrise	2004	Canon EOS 10D	RAW	Tokina 28-70mm f/2.8	1/25 sec.	f/11	100
63	"Early Morning Riser" / North Campus Loggia after Sunrise	2004	Canon EOS 10D	RAW	Canon 20-35mm f/3.5-4.5	1/15 sec.	f/11	100
64	Clark Hall on a Winter Morning	2004	Canon EOS 10D	RAW	Canon 20-35mm f/3.5-4.5	1/50 sec.	f/11	100
65	North Campus Loggia on a Winter Night	2004	Canon EOS 10D	RAW	Tokina 28-70mm f/2.8	2.5 seconds	f/8	200
66	Smith Annex & Langan at Night	2006	Canon EOS 10D	RAW	Canon 24mm f/3.5 L T/S	10 seconds	f/11	400
67	Gates Tower in Snowfall at Night	2005	Canon EOS 10D	RAW	Canon 24mm f/3.5 L T/S	10 seconds	f/8	400
68	North Campus Winter	2005	Canon EOS 10D	RAW	Canon 70-200 f/2.8 L	2 seconds	f/9	400
69	Darby Gym (Razed 2004)	2004	Canon EOS 10D	JPEG	Tokina 28-70mm f/2.8	1/125 sec.	f/7.1	100
70	South Campus Trees & Haines Hall	2005	Canon EOS 10D	RAW	Canon 28-135mm f/3.5-5.6 Image Stabilized	1/40 sec.	f/8	200
71	South Campus Coneflowers	2005	Canon EOS 10D	RAW	Canon 70-200mm f/2.8 L	1/30 sec.	f/9	100
72	Late Afternoon Light on South Campus	2005	Canon EOS 10D	RAW	Canon 24-70mm f/2.8 L	1/6 sec.	f/16	100
73	Lazier Hall in Spring	2004	Canon EOS 10D	JPEG	Tokina 28-70mm f/2.8	1/400 sec.	f/7.1	100
74	East Campus Loggia #1	2004	Canon EOS Elan 7	Fujichrome Sensia (E-6)	Zenitar 16mm f/2.8 Fisheye	unknown	unknown	100
75	East Campus Loggia #2	2004	Canon EOS 10D	RAW	Canon 20-35mm f/3.5-4.5	1/40 sec.	f/8	100
76	Coneflowers and Bucksbaum	2005	Canon EOS 10D	RAW	Canon 24-70mm f/2.8 L	1/160 sec.	f/8	100
77	Bucksbaum & "Morphosis"	2005	Canon EOS 10D	RAW	Tokina 12-24mm f/4	1/20 sec.	f/22	100
78	Herrick Chapel	2004	Canon EOS 10D	RAW	Canon 20-35mm f/3.5-4.5	1/40 sec.	f/8	200
79	Trees, Benches and Noyce	2005	Canon EOS 10D	RAW	Canon 24-70mm f/2.8 L	1/30 sec.	f/11	100
80	"Alpha and Omega" Sundial and Coneflowers	2004	Canon EOS 10D	RAW	Tokina 28-70mm f/2.8	1/25 sec.	f/9	100
81	Darby Gym in Winter	2004	Canon EOS D30	JPEG	Tokina 28-70mm f/2.8	1/320 sec.	f/8	200
82	Bucksbaum Fire Exit	2005	Canon EOS 10D	RAW	Canon 24mm f/3.5 L T/S	1/3 sec.	f/16	400

Plate 82 - Bucksbaum Fire Exit

Colophon

A Portrait of Grinnell

The Architecture and Landscape of Grinnell College

Published by 100 Books Publishing Company
Printed in China by Regent Publishing Services Limited

The typeface for *A Portrait of Grinnell* is Garamond

www.david-kennedy.com

dk@david-kennedy.com

ISBN: 0-9763765-4-7